Dinosaurs in Wellies

'Dinosaurs in Wellies'
An original concept by Lou Treleaven
© Lou Treleaven

Illustrated by Paul Nicholls

Published by MAVERICK ARTS PUBLISHING LTD
Studio 11, City Business Centre, 6 Brighton Road,
Horsham, West Sussex, RH13 5BB
© Maverick Arts Publishing Limited August 2020
+44 (0)1403 256941

A CIP catalogue record for this book is available at the British Library.

ISBN 978-1-84886-682-9

www.maverickbooks.co.uk

This book is rated as: Blue Band (Guided Reading)
This story is mostly decodable at Letters and Sounds Phase 4.
Up to five non-decodable story words are included.

Dinosaurs in Wellies

by **Lou Treleaven**
illustrated by **Paul Nicholls**

Stomp loved his wellies.

He had a LOT of pairs.

He loved them all!

He had wellies on when he got up,
and when he went to bed.

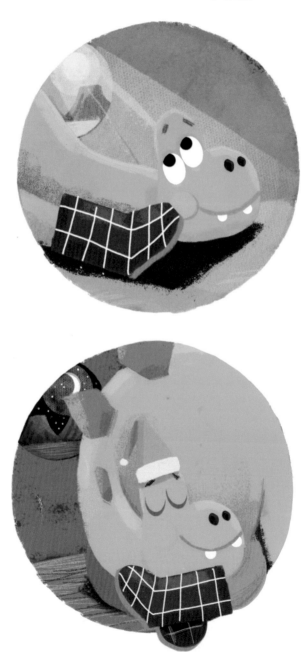

He had wellies on when he went out.

"You cannot come in with wellies on, Stomp," said Dad.

So Stomp put on his Slipper Wellies.

"You cannot come in with wellies on, Stomp," said Miss Rex.

So Stomp put on his Thinking Wellies.

"You cannot run in wellies," said Thump.

So Stomp put on his Quick Wellies.

Stomp loved to get wellies as a present.

"I wish I could use all my wellies at once!" said Stomp.

One morning, it started to rain hard.

"My feet are getting wet," said Dad.

The rain went on all morning.

At lunch, it was still raining.

The rain went on all night!

Next morning, there was a BIG problem.

"There is far too much rain!"

said Miss Rex.

"We will cross the river and go to the top of the hill," Miss Rex said.

"I can help!" said Stomp.

Dad and Stomp went to get his wellies.

Stomp handed all his wellies out.

There were no wellies left for Stomp.

"How will I get across the river?"

he said.

"We will help you!" said Miss Rex.

Quiz

1. Stomp loved his...
a) Hats
b) Tail
c) Wellies

2. What wellies did Stomp put on to run?
a) His Thinking Wellies
b) His Quick Wellies
c) His Sporty Wellies

3. What did Stomp wish for?
a) To have wellies in all colours
b) To use all his wellies at once
c) To climb the mountain in wellies

4. There was far too much…

a) Rain

b) Sun

c) Snow

5. What did Stomp do to help?

a) He kept his wellies for himself

b) He handed all his wellies out

c) He drank all the water

Turn over for answers

Book Bands for Guided Reading

The Institute of Education book banding system is a scale of colours that reflects the various levels of reading difficulty. The bands are assigned by taking into account the content, the language style, the layout and phonics. Word, phrase and sentence level work is also taken into consideration.

Maverick Early Readers are a bright, attractive range of books covering the pink to white bands. All of these books have been book banded for guided reading to the industry standard and edited by a leading educational consultant.

To view the whole Maverick Readers scheme, visit our website at

www.maverickearlyreaders.com

Or scan the QR code above to view our scheme instantly!

Quiz Answers: 1c, 2b, 3b, 4a, 5b